Design Goods Showcase

Published by BNN, Inc.
1-20-6, Ebisu-minami, Shibuya-ku, Tokyo,
150-0022, Japan
fax: +81-3-5725-1511
e-mail: info@bnn.co.jp
www.bnn.co.jp

Art Direction & Design : Takahito Ishida (NAIJEL GRAPH)
Photo : Seiji Mizuno
Cookie Design [Cover, Chapter title page] : cookieboy
Translation [Foreword] : R.I.C. Publications
Editing : Sayaka Ishii

Publisher : Kouichi Yabuuchi

Printing & Binding : KOSAIDO Co., Ltd.

ISBN978-4-86100-735-4
Printed in Japan

Design Goods Showcase
夢みるデザインプロダクト

はじめに

「プロダクト」と聞くと、規格化された電化製品や、モダンなインテリア家具などを思い浮かべがち
ですが、この本で取り上げるのは、デザイナーやアーティストによるグラフィックを生かした商品や、
自然を象った温もりのある作品など。

作家のつくるもの、デザイナーのつくるもの、メーカーのつくるもの、これらをひとくくりにして「プ
ロダクト」と呼ぶことは稀かもしれませんが、新しいものづくりの胎動は、こうした各々の営みを
通して、紡ぎ出されるものだと考えます。

多くの人が、日常に流れる時間の中で、心地よい造形に触れ、それを選びとる行為を、とても大切
にしています。心が躍るプロダクトとの巡り合いは、まさに夢みる瞬間です。

誰かの手に渡るとき、それぞれのアイテムがもたらすファンタジーを、ぜひ想像しながらご一読く
ださい。

Foreword

The word "products" may remind you of standardized electrical appliances or modern-looking
interior furniture. This book, however, introduces "products" such as graphic design goods and
heartwarming nature-shaped work created by designers or artists.

It may not be normal to lump such masterpieces of designers or creators work with
manufacturers' merchandize and categorize uniformly as products. But I believe that up-to-date
creations can be woven and brought to life through various production techniques.

A lot of people place great value on appreciating and selecting artistic products in everyday life.
Encountering a fascinating product can be a dreamful experience if you let your imagination
wander.

How exciting it can be to imagine a world of fantasy that each of these products has. I really do
hope that you enjoy this book and the pleasure that it will bring you.

Contents

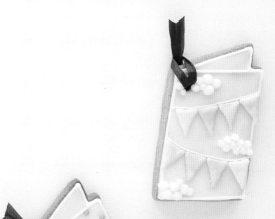

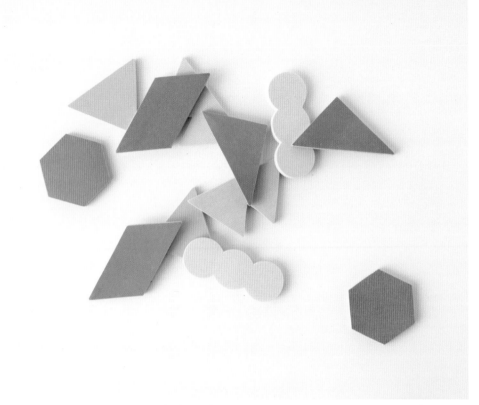

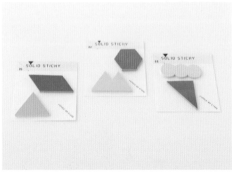

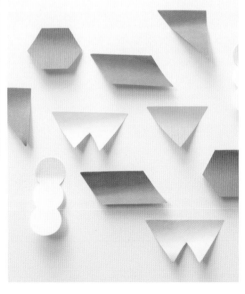

STICKY - SOLID STICKY

Brand : SPACE-BA store   Designer : Kyoyoung Lee   http://www.spacebastore.com/

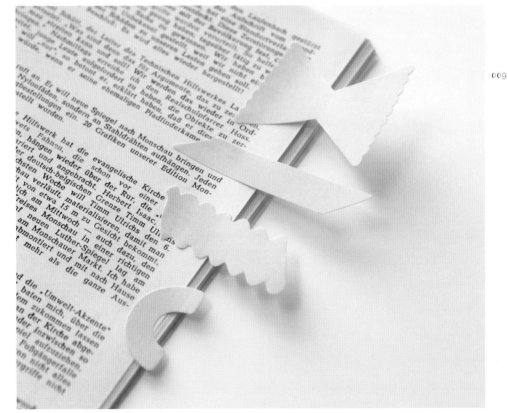

STICKY - pasta it

http://www.spacebastore.com   Designer : Kyoyoung Lee   Brand : SPACE-BA store

STICKY - fusen （フセン）
Brand / Designer : drop around　http://www.droparound.com/, http://www.classiky.co.jp/

012

TAPE MEASURE, PINCUSHION - メジャー〈machibari〉, ピンクッション〈Rice lace, machibari〉

Brand : cocca   Designer : FLANGE × cocca   http://www.cocca.ne.jp/

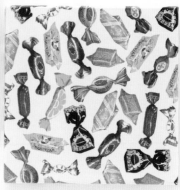

BOX - BOX FRAME, macaroon M, LETTER BOX   http://boxandneedle.com

Brand : BOX & NEEDLE   Designer: 大西景子 Keiko Onishi, 夏目奈央子 Natsume Naoko, 伏見雪子 Fushimi Setsuko

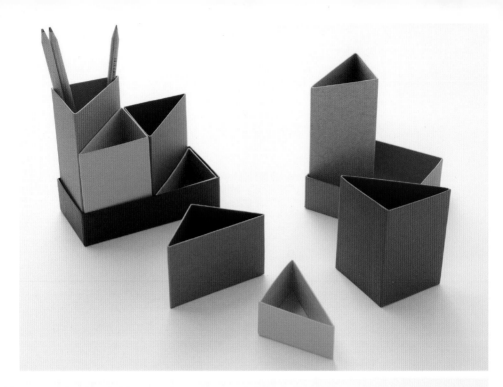

BOX - PENTATE SISTERS, SUVAKO 3   http://boxandneedle.com

Brand : BOX & NEEDLE   Designer: 大西景子 Keiko Onishi, 夏目奈央子 Natsume Naoko, 伏見雪子 Fushimi Setsuko

http://boxandneedle.com **BOX - KNOW WHO**

Designer: 大西景子 Keiko Onishi, 夏目奈央子 Natsume Naoko, 伏見雪子 Fushimi Setsuko Brand : BOX & NEEDLE

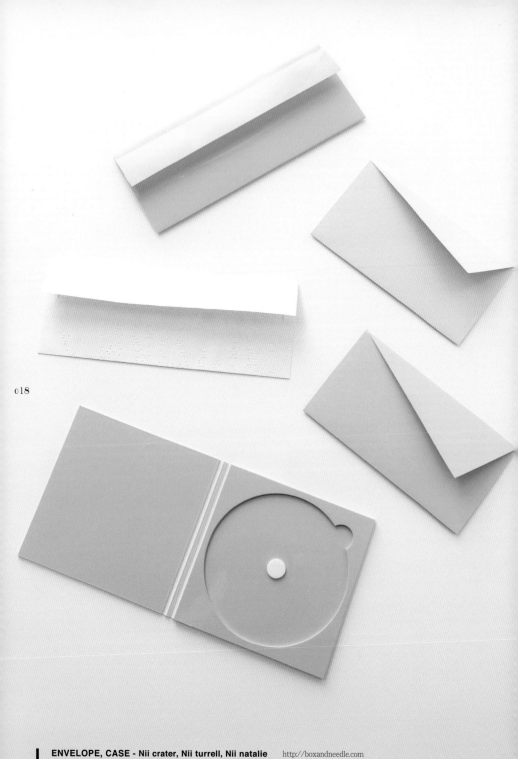

018

ENVELOPE, CASE - Nii crater, Nii turrell, Nii natalie   http://boxandneedle.com

Brand : BOX & NEEDLE   Designer: 大西景子 Keiko Onishi, 夏目奈央子 Natsume Naoko, 伏見雪子 Fushimi Setsuko

PEN CASE - 赤青ペンケース 55 - **Red&Blue55 Pencil Case,** 折れ線ペンケース **Line Graph Pencil Case**

http://www.yuruliku.com/　　Designer : 池上幸志 Koushi Ikegami,　オオネダキヌエ Kinue Oneda　　Brand : yuruliku

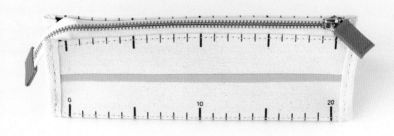

PEN CASE - SanSuke ペンケース **Triangular Scale Pencil Case,** 上履きペンケース **Sole Pencil Case**

Brand : yuruliku   Designer : 池上幸志 Koushi Ikegami, オオネダキヌエ Kinue Oneda   http://www.yuruliku.com/

CASE - 三角ケース Triangle Box

http://www.yuruliku.com/   Designer : 池上幸志 Koushi Ikegami, オオネダキヌエ Kinue Oneda   Brand : yuruliku

022

WRAPPING PAPER - Gift Wrap ⟨Tag black/gold , Tag red/silver⟩

Brand : Number 62   Designer : Bob Foundation   http://www.number62.jp/, http://www.bobfoundation.com/

Nº 62

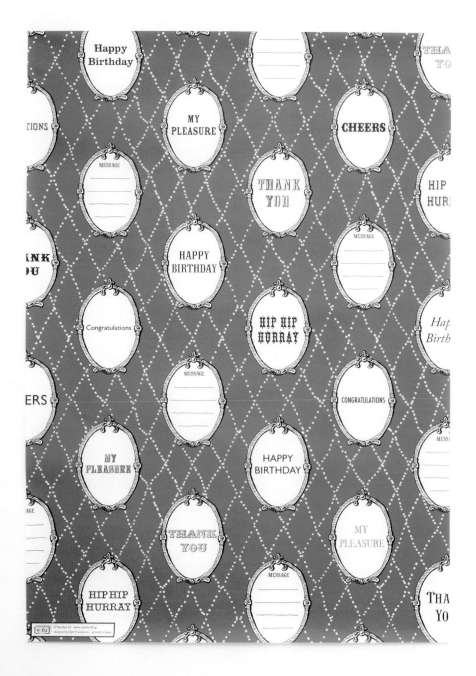

WRAPPING PAPER - Gift Wrap 〈message green , message blue〉

Brand : Number 62　　Designer : Bob Foundation　　http://www.number62.jp/, http://www.bobfoundation.com/

026

CARD - Message Card

http://www.number62.jp/, http://www.bobfoundation.com/   Designer : Bob Foundation   Brand : Number 62

CARD - Gift Card

Brand : Number 62   Designer : Bob Foundation   http://www.number62.jp/, http://www.bobfoundation.com/

MESSAGE BOX WITH CANDLE - Decoration Letter

Brand : Titto   Designer : 南 英樹 Hideki Minami, 望月麻子 Asako Mochizuki, 千葉美咲 Misaki Chiba   http://www.titto.info/

LIGHT
IN YOUR HEART

Titto®

*Light
in your heart*

Titto®

032

CARD - Spaceman Card 〈Kinder, Owl, Hippie, Vampire, Forest〉
Brand : mmmg / millimeter milligram   Designer : OH HYUN SUK   http://jposh.jp/, http://mmmg.net/

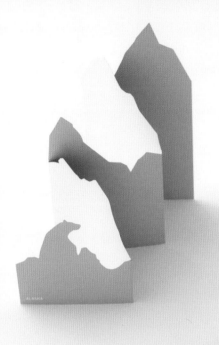

CARD, NOTE BOOK - Landscape Card, Note Class, Plan

http://jposh.jp/, http://mmmg.net/   Designer : OH HYUN SUK   Brand : mmmg / millimeter milligram

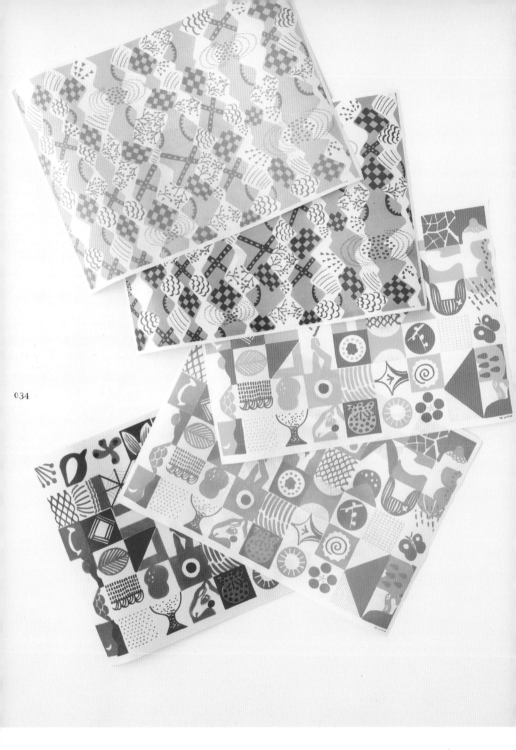

034

PAPER - Natsuko KOZUE paper〈畑，手と手，森，熱帯植物〉
Designer：楠 夏子 Natsuko KOZUE   http://www17.ocn.ne.jp/~cozupy/

BOOK JACKET - Natsuko KOZUE bookcover "trip" series
Designer：楢 夏子 Natsuko KOZUE   http://www17.ocn.ne.jp/~cozupy/

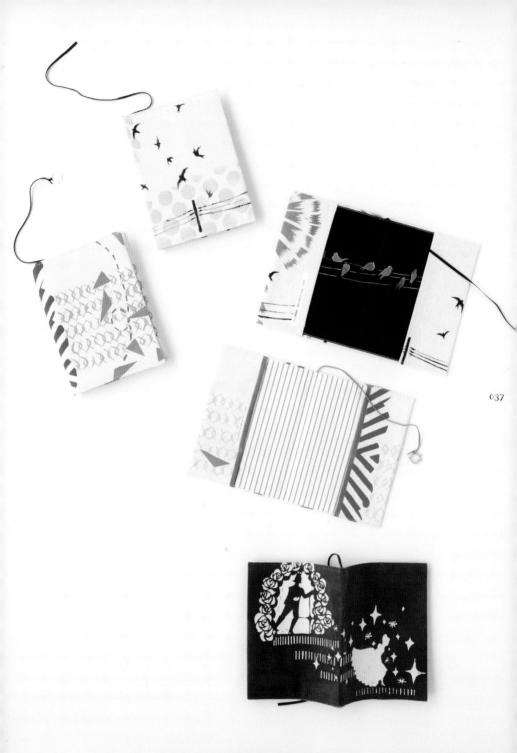

BOOK JACKET - Natsuko KOZUE bookcover 〈ツバメ , airport, シンデレラ〉

http://www17.ocn.ne.jp/~cozupy/   Designer : 梢 夏子 Natsuko KOZUE

NOTEBOOK - 神坂雪佳著「海路」てぬぐいノート（小）
Brand：株式会社アーテファクトリー　Artefactory INC.　　Designer：アートショップ・ピエボ　art shop pievo

039

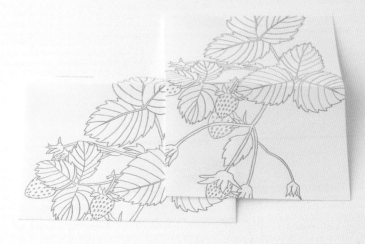

CARD, ENVELOPE - 封筒と二つ折りカードのセット〈葉イチゴ , イチゴ〉
Brand : tokyo paradise   Designer : 川島枝梨花 Erica kawashima   http://tokyoparadise.jp/

CARD, ENVELOPE - 封筒と二つ折りカードのセット〈ぶどう , すみれ〉
http://tokyoparadise.jp/　　Designer：川島枝梨花　Erica kawashima　　Brand : tokyo paradise

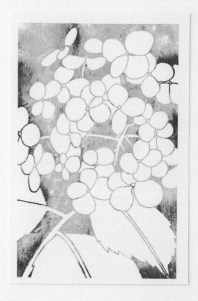

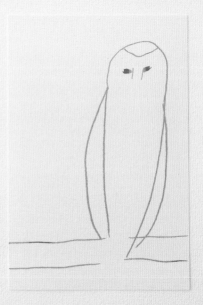

POSTCARD - 郵便はがき〈ゆり（シェルピンク），あじさい，つるむらさき，フクロウ（青目）〉
Brand : tokyo paradise　　Designer : 川島枝梨花 Erica kawashima　　http://tokyoparadise.jp/

秋明菊

POSTCARD - 郵便はがき〈たんぽぽ，ハイビスカス，秋明菊，萩〉

http://tokyoparadise.jp/ 　　Designer : 川島枝梨花 Erica kawashima 　　Brand : tokyo paradise

ENVELOPE - 折水引 ORIMIZUHIKI
Brand：かみの工作所　　Designer：大友 学 gaku otomo　　http://www.gakudesign.jp/

045

CARD - PIECE OF CAKE CARD

http://o-ono.jp/   Designer：オオノ・マユミ　Mayumi OONO   Brand：かみの工作所

Photo Credit : Nendesign

MESSAGE CARD - Face Card

Brand : Nendesign   Designer : 吉田芳洋 Yoshihiro Yoshida, 菊池志帆 Shiho Kikuchi   http://www.nendesign.net/

CLIP, STICKY - CLIP CREATURES, Sticky Notes : PIGEON

http://twelvetone.jp/   Designer : 角田 崇 Takashi Tsunoda   Brand : twelvetone

LETTER PAPER & ENVELOPE, ORIGAMI - レターセット，おりがみ
Designer：やまさき薫　Kaoru Yamasaki　http://www.gruescope.com/, http://yamasakikaoru.blog113.fc2.com/

edited photographs 1992–2004

BOOKMARK - Slept Between The Pages
http://www.utrecht.jp/   Brand / Designer : UTRECHT

LETTER PAPER & ENVELOPE - たて書きの手紙, よこ書きの手紙

Brand：かみみの　　Designer：柏木江里子　　http://www.kamimino.jp/, http://kashiwa-gi.com/

THEY CALLED
HER STYRENE

BOOKMARK - 羽根箋

http://www5d.biglobe.ne.jp/~calico/10-trill/trill-00top.htm　　Designer：ユカワアツコ Atsuko Yukawa　　Brand：トリル

052

STICKY - GreenMarker®   http://www.yuruliku.com/, http://www.yuruliku.com/greenmarker/
Brand : yuruliku   Designer : 池上幸志 Koushi Ikegami, オオネダキヌエ Kinue Oneda

Dick Higgins
P. O. Box 688
Newhall. Ca 91321

Kalifornien
23. April 1970

H. Isaac
Vorsitzender
ROUNDSCHAU/BILD PLASTIK
5108 Monschau
WEST GERMANY

Sehr geehrter Herr Isaac,

Schöner Dank auf der Einladung und auch auf den
Photographen für Ihre Ausstellung. Leider ist Ihr Brief
erst heute angekommen. Deshalb ist es, ich glaube, ganz
unmöglich, daß ich ein kompliziertes Werk hinschicken oder
dort darstellen lassen darf. Ich bin zu spät. Dafur.

Aber trotzdem ich habe ein Konzept, das meine
Ideen repräsentieren dürfte. Genau um Mitternacht soll
jemand hinkommen, bei einem Stuck oder Kunstwerk, und
ganz schnell die Hosen fallen lasen und den nackten
Arsch ganz kurzer Zeit ausstellen. In diesem Augenblick
soll ein Lichtbildner ganz schnell mit einer Blitzlampe
eine Aufnahme machen. Und dann ist alles am Abends
fertig bis zum nächsten Abend. Die Leute die hinkommen
sollen alle merkwürdige Leute sein, ob in der Nähe oder
ganz berühmt durch Deutschland oder die Welt, oder in
der Kunstwelt. Aber besonders in den Photos, es ist wichtig
das man keine Gesichte sehen soll. Man muß nur die Anonymität
der anderen präsentieren, trotzdem daß der sehr okasionele
Zushauer die Leute erkennt, und auch muß dieses auch eine
Ausnahme sein, denn das Licht muß (wie die Aufnahme) ganz
wirksam und leistungsfähig befertigt ergänzt.

Am Letzten Tag der Ausstellung dürfen alle Aufnahmen
hingestellt werden, aber trotzdem ganz ohne ausweise. Vielleicht
hat man eine Aufnahme gesehen: er soll nicht bei der Aufnahme
das berühmten Leut erkennen, weder beim machen noch beim
Silberdruck. Photodruck. Was glauben Sie, Herr Isaac.
Können Sie es machen?

Hochachtungsvoll, und mit freundlichsten Grußen,

Dick Higgins

MESSAGE CARD - ティー・フォー・トゥー **Tea for two**
Brand：マーブル・アンド・コー　MARBLE & Co.　　http://www.marble-and-co.com/

055

PEN - フルール ローズ, フルール ダリア
Brand : マーブル・アンド・コー MARBLE & Co.

CARD - フォトフレームカード **Photo Frame Card**
Brand : sallbo design   Designer : Sally Kubo-Starr   http://www.sallbo.com/, http://sallboshop.com/

057

CARD - リングコースターカード（誕生石＋ゴールドダイアモンド）**Ring Coaster Card（Birthstones＋Diamond Gold Ring）**

http://www.sallbo.com/, http://sallboshop.com/　　Designer : Sally Kubo-Starr　　Brand : sallbo design

STICKY, CARD - 付箋メモ **Post It Notes,** ハートバルーンカード **Heart Balloon Card**
Brand : sallbo design   Designer : Sally Kubo-Starr   http://www.sallbo.com/, http://sallboshop.com/

http://jposh.jp/, http://www.o-check.net/   **NOTEBOOK - Note. Small , The Diary Version 3 Small, Note**
Designer : CHO SOO JUNG   Brand : o-check design graphics / SPRING COME, RAIN FALL INC.

VOYAGE AGRÉABLE
L'INFINIE IMMENSITÉ DES ESPACES QUE J'IGNORE ET QUI M'IGNORENT

r i o r
u c t s

SUGAR BOWL - 鳩の砂糖壷

Brand：栄屋工芸店　　http://www.landscape-products.net/archives/2008/09/post_1.html

TOOTHPICK HOLDER - 鳩の爪楊枝入れ

http://www.landscape-products.net/archives/2008/09/post_2.html　　Brand：栄屋工芸店

066

CERAMIC - peacock：grey L/S
Brand：バーズワーズ BIRDS' WORDS　　Designer：伊藤利江 Rie Ito　　http://www.birds-words.com/

CERAMIC - wall bird : blue XS/S/M/L/XL

Brand : バーズワーズ BIRDS' WORDS   Designer : 伊藤利江 Rie Ito   http://www.birds-words.com/

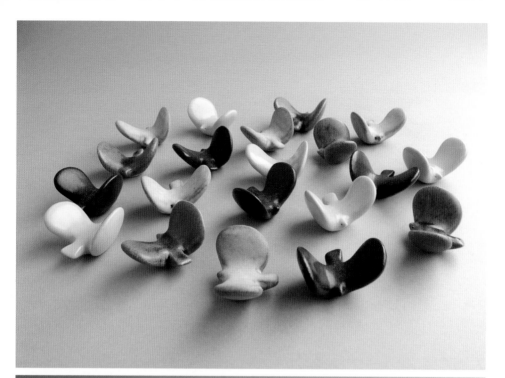

CERAMIC - bird rests, oval bird：yellow S/M/L

http://www.birds-words.com/　　Designer：伊藤利江 Rie Ito　　Brand：バーズワーズ BIRDS' WORDS

CERAMIC - buttons, brooches
Brand : バーズワーズ BIRDS' WORDS   Designer : 伊藤利江 Rie Ito   http://www.birds-words.com/

BONSAI - 苔盆栽 はりねずみ , ひつじ , ひなどり **includes moss**

http://www.nousaku.co.jp/   Designer：青木有理子 yuriko aoki   Brand：能作 NOUSAKU

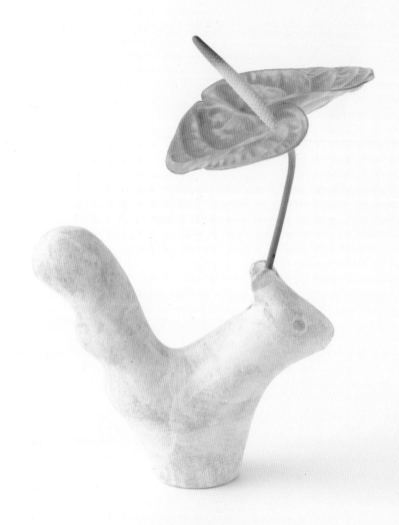

072

CERAMIC VASE - リス , 仔リス
Brand : atelier de la paix   Designer : 鹿児島 睦 Makoto Kagoshima   http://homepage.mac.com/makoto46/

CERAMIC WARE - クジャク，花の器

Brand : atelier de la paix　　Designer : 鹿児島 睦　Makoto Kagoshima　　http://homepage.mac.com/makoto46/

CERAMIC TILE - タイル / 青い花シリーズ

http://homepage.mac.com/makoto46/   Designer：鹿児島 睦 Makoto Kagoshima   Brand : atelier de la paix

CERAMIC PLATE - The Garden as Science Fiction / Leaf Dish
Brand : ON ZA LINE   Designer : 小玉清美 Kiyomi Kodama, 倉橋 愛 Ai Kurahashi   http://www.onzaline.com/

078

CERAMIC VASE - The Garden as Science Fiction / Flower Vase, Root Flower Vase
Brand : ON ZA LINE   Designer : 小玉清美 Kiyomi Kodama, 倉橋 愛 Ai Kurahashi   http://www.onzaline.com/

COASTER - Letter Coasters
Brand : Little Factory   Designer : Chifun Wong   http://littlefactory.com, http://the-item.com

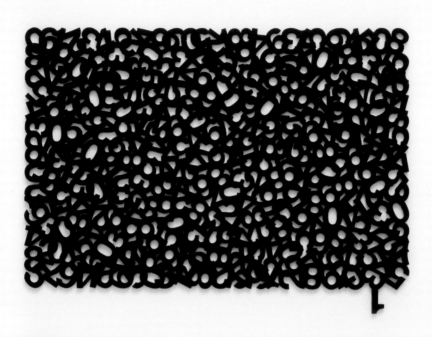

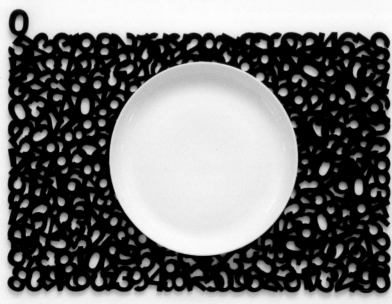

PLACEMAT - Number Placemats

http://littlefactory.com, http://the-item.com   Designer : Chifun Wong   Brand : Little Factory

CUP & SAUCER - カップ＆ソーサー **READY OR NOT?**
Brand : THOUSAND LEAVES　　Designer : 谷田 浩　Hiroshi Tanida, 御徒町理理　Riri Okachimachi　　http://www.thousandleaves.jp/

GLASS - リスコップ，ねこっぷ，うさこっぷ
Designer : 土井朋子　Tomoko Doi　　http://www.doitomo.com/

086

WOODEN DOLL - キコオリジナルこけし
Brand：キコ　QUICO　　http://www.quico.jp

087

CERAMIC PLATE - レースのお皿

http://po-to-bo.com   Designer : 島田知子 Tomoko Shimada   Brand : po-to-bo

088

CHOPSTICK REST - シロクマの熊五郎，ペンギンの銀さん 2 号

Brand：楽土　Raku-do　　Designer：多田誠三　Seizo Tada　　http://raku-do.net/, http://shop.raku-do.net/

SMALL CUP - シロクマの熊五郎お猪口１号，２号

http://raku-do.net/, http://shop.raku-do.net/　　Designer：多田誠三　Seizo Tada　　Brand：楽土　Raku-do

090

GLASS - "suii" NORTHPOLE and SOUTHPOLE
Brand : cocoo natural home decor   Designer : 角田恵理 Eri Tsunoda   http://cocoo.jp

ORNAMENT - "motion catcher" 〈**FRISBEE DOG, ape**〉

Brand : cocoo natural home decor   Designer : 角田恵理 Eri Tsunoda   http://cocoo.jp

093

ORNAMENT - かみふうせん・くも

http://www.kamimino.jp, http://yo-happy.com　　Designer：のぐちようこ　　Brand：かみみの

094

ORNAMENT - つながるはた・ふかふかさんかく, つながるわっか・まる
Brand：かみみの　　Designer：のぐちようこ　　http://www.kamimino.jp, http://yo-happy.com

CERAMIC BOWL - 富士ちゃわん，赤富士ちゃわん
Designer : 猿式箱 Sarushikibako http://www.sarushiki.com/

098

CERAMIC WARE - YACCO WARI, YACCO TURANARI   http://www.e-kihara.co.jp/
Brand : 有田HOUEN / 株式会社キハラ ARITA HOUEN / KIHARA INC.   Designer : 高橋 正 Tadashi Takahashi

CUSHION - Cushion with buttons
Brand : Tas-ka   Designer : Jantien Baas, Hester Worst   http://www.tas-ka.nl/, http://www.collectedbytas-ka.com/

TRAY, TEA COSY - Dinnertray , Tea Cosy

http://www.tas-ka.nl/, http://www.collectedbytas-ka.com/   Designer : Jantien Baas, Hester Worst   Brand : Tas-ka

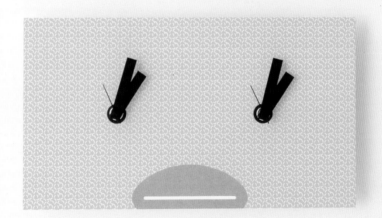

CLOCK - 24 Graphics
Brand : Nendesign   Designer : 吉田芳洋 Yoshihiro Yoshida, 菊池志帆 Shiho Kikuchi   http://www.nendesign.net

103

http://www.gba-project.com/, http://www.maq.co.jp/ **TRASH BAG - Love it！君マナーバッグ**

Designer：（CD）山阪佳彦 Yoshihiko Yamasaka, （AD）瀬古晋也 Shinya Seko　Brand：GARBAGE BAG ART WORK / MAQ inc.

BLANKET - レイニーデイ ブランケット **BLANKETS RAINYDAY**
Brand / Designer : ドナ・ウィルソン DONNA WILSON   http://www.bytrico.com/designer_label/donnawilson.html

105

GLASS, CUSHION - ワンダーランド **WONDERLAND GLASS,** カッドリークラウド **CUDDLY CLOUDS**

http://www.bytrico.com/designer_label/donnawilson.html　　Brand / Designer：ドナ・ウィルソン　DONNA WILSON

106

LAMP - メグスリの木 ペンダントランプ
Brand : cocca　　　Designer : Object work hobo × cocca　　　http://www.cocca.ne.jp/

LAMP - チューリップランプ

http://www.cocca.ne.jp/   Designer : raquel meller   Brand : cocca

FRAME - Framed Objects

Brand : the.   Designer : Mihoko Ouchi   http://www.thinkofthe.com

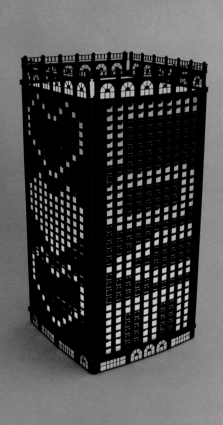

LED CANDLE LIGHT - DOT ART BUILDING

http://twelvetone.jp   Designer : 角田 崇 Takashi Tsunoda   Brand : twelvetone

110

LED CANDLE LIGHT - はなあかり
Brand：かみみの　　Designer：磯野梨影　　http://www.kamimino.jp, http://pear-ds.com

Photo Credit：冨田里美

http://www.torafu.com/　**PAPER PRODUCTS -** 空気の器　**air vase**

Designer：鈴野浩一　Koichi Suzuno, 禿真哉　Shinya Kamuro　　Brand：株式会社 トラフ建築設計事務所　TORAFU ARCHITECTS Inc.

TABLECLOTH - Photo Print series / Table cloth _ study

Brand / Designer : Orange tip   http://www.orangetip.net/

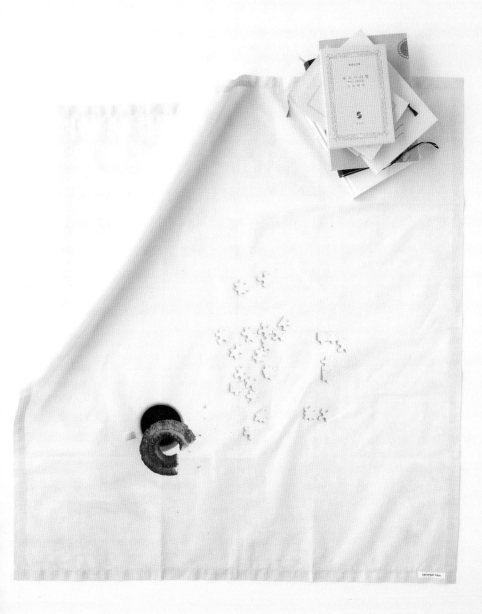

113

TABLECLOTH - Photo Print series / Table cloth _ coffee break
http://www.orangetip.net/   Brand / Designer : Orange tip

114

TOWEL - SUMAU BASE / リバーシブルのほそながタオル **SA-SA**

Brand : SUMAU nani IRO   Designer : SUMAU Design Team   http://www.kokka.co.jp/sumau/, http://www.itonao.com/

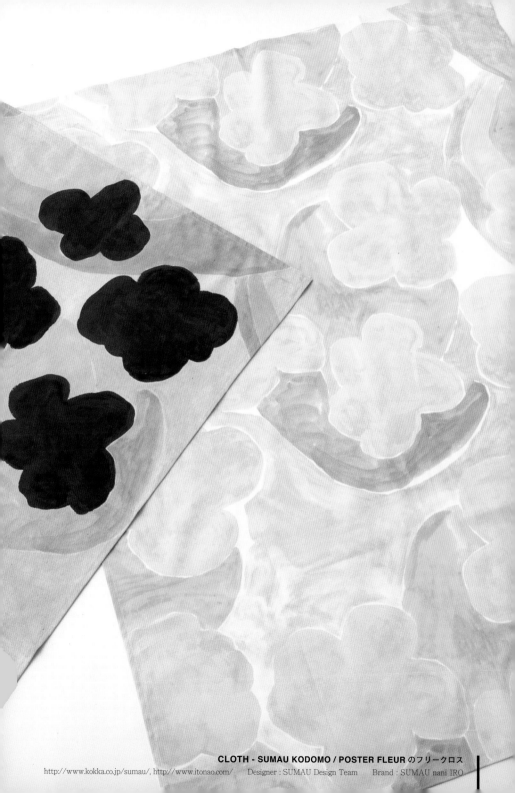

CLOTH - SUMAU KODOMO / POSTER FLEUR のフリークロス

http://www.kokka.co.jp/sumau/, http://www.itonao.com/   Designer : SUMAU Design Team   Brand : SUMAU nani IRO

116

118

CANVAS - PLAY PLAY PLAY

Brand : amabro   Designer : 村上 周 MURAKAMI AMANE   http://www.amabro.com, http://www.amdr.jp/

PLATE - soil -pastel-

http://www.amabro.com, http://www.amdr.jp/　　Designer：村上 周　MURAKAMI AMANE　　Brand：amabro

120

SMALL CUP - CHOKU 青磁 , 藤花
Brand : amabro   Designer : 村上 周 MURAKAMI AMANE   http://www.amabro.com, http://www.amdr.jp/

SMALL PLATE - MAME

http://www.amabro.com, http://www.amdr.jp/   Designer：村上 周 MURAKAMI AMANE   Brand : amabro

122

SMALL TEACUP - BAB-CUP

Brand : amabro   Designer : 村上 周 MURAKAMI AMANE   http://www.amabro.com, http://www.amdr.jp/

TEA CADDY - IVANA helsinki + collex オリジナル紅茶缶

http://shop.collex.jp/?mode=grp&gid=76297   Designer：Paola Suhonen   Brand : IVANA helsinki

TEXTILE - forest ⟨昼, 夕⟩
Brand : cocca   http://www.cocca.ne.jp/

TEXTILE - 流星ボーダー〈ゴールド, ピューター〉
Brand : cocca   Designer : コウモリヤ   http://www.cocca.ne.jp/

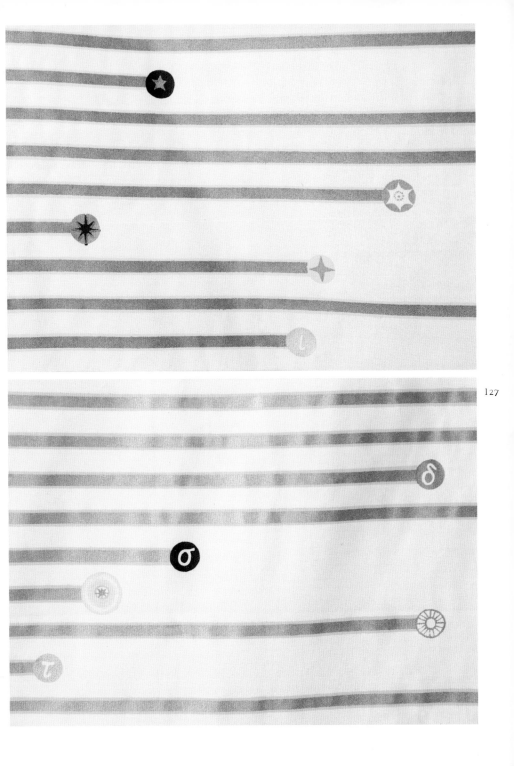

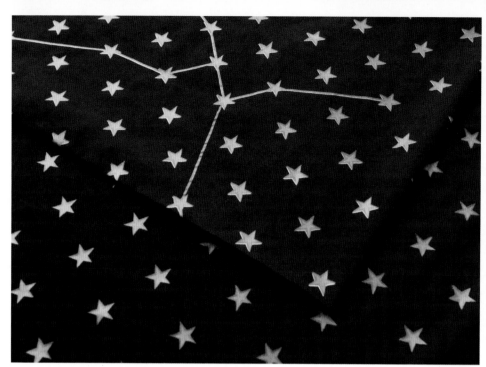

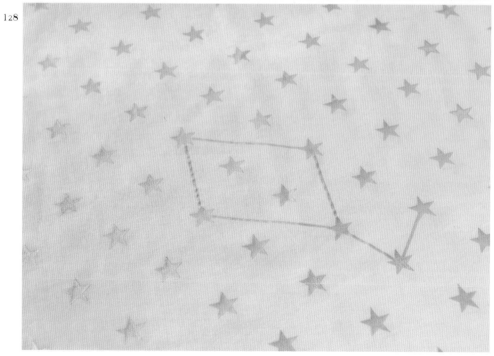

TEXTILE - 星ドット〈夜 , 昼〉
Brand : cocca   Designer : コウモリヤ   http://www.cocca.ne.jp/

129

CANDLE - フロストピラー Frostpillar

http://progressivecandle.blog21.fc2.com/ Designer：福井優子 Brand：プログレッシヴ キャンドル Progressive Candle

SOAP - EBISOAP 〈GREECE, New York, Netherland, SWEDEN, NIPPON〉

Brand：ライフスタイルブランド EBI   Designer：平松創三 SOZO HIRAMATSU   http://ebidesign.jp/, http://ishin95.exblog.jp/

131

132

CANDLE - FRANKINCENSE, FANTASY, COCO, FUR

Brand：ライフスタイルブランド EBI   Designer：平松創三 SOZO HIRAMATSU   http://ebidesign.jp/, http://ishin95.exblog.jp/

TEXTILE - 北の模様帖〈森 mori〉

Brand：点と線模様製作所 ten to sen   Designer：岡理恵子 Rieko Oka   http://www.tentosen.info

TEXTILE - 北の模様帖〈紫陽花 hydrangea〉
Brand：点と線模様製作所 ten to sen　　Designer：岡理恵子 Rieko Oka　　http://www.tentosen.info

TEXTILE - 北の模様帖〈道ばた roadside〉
Brand：点と線模様製作所 ten to sen　Designer：岡理恵子 Rieko Oka　http://www.tentosen.info

shion

ods

BROOCH - 刺繍ブローチ

Brand : HIPOTA　　Designer：廣田 薫 Kaoru Hirota　　http://www8.plala.or.jp/hipotastitch/

143

144

BROOCH - 動物ブローチ

Brand : ai   Designer：布川愛子 fukawa aiko   http://www.nice-nice-nice.com

146

TIE - クラシックポップ
Brand : giraffe　　Designer：黒沢秋乃　Akino Kurosawa　　http://www.giraffe-tie.com

147

TIE - 蛍光チェック，ウールボーダーニット

http://www.giraffe-tie.com　　Designer : 中村裕子　Yuco Nakamura　　Brand : giraffe

148

TIE - ウールドットレジメン

Brand : giraffe　　Designer : 中村裕子　Yuco Nakamura　　http://www.giraffe-tie.com

149

TIE, BOW TIE - ウエスタンフリンジ , コーデュロイ蝶タイ

http://www.giraffe-tie.com　　Designer：黒沢秋乃　Akino Kurosawa, 中村裕子　Yuco Nakamura　　Brand：giraffe

150

UMBRELLA - 晴雨兼用傘　カボチャ〈シンデレラ〉

http://www.cocca.ne.jp/　　Designer : DiCesare　　Brand : cocca

152

BUTTON - 刺繍ボタン〈桜粒の雨 , 橙灯草 , 遠樹の奏 , 蒼春の鳥 , 星文ノ原 , 音星盤〉

Brand / Designer : petitricot　　http://www.5f.biglobe.ne.jp/~p-tricot/

BUTTON - 刺繍ボタン〈墨縞の灯，季染敷き，水鈴の雫，織りならび＜綾鳥＞栗染め，黄敷の譜，白凪の景〉

http://www5f.biglobe.ne.jp/~p-tricot/　　Brand / Designer : petitricot

BAG - ルナバッグ **Luna Bag**
Brand：ドーサ dosa　　Designer：クリスティーナ・キム Christina Kim　　http://www.quico.jp

POUCH - IVANA helsinki StarRain Series 〈ポーチ L、ポーチ S〉

Brand : IVANA helsinki　　Designer：Paola Suhonen　　http://shop.collex.jp/?mode=grp&gid=76297

BAG - IVANA helsinki StarRain Series 〈バッグ〉

http://shop.collex.jp/?mode=grp&gid=76297   Designer：Paola Suhonen   Brand : IVANA helsinki

158

CERAMIC BROOCH - リボンブローチ
Brand : po-to-bo   Designer : 島田知子 Tomoko Shimada   http://po-to-bo.com

RING, BOW TIE - リング〈ビッグパール , チョゴリゴールド〉, 蝶ネクタイ〈チェック柄 , ギザギザストライプ , 濃×白ボーダー〉

http://ebidesign.jp/, http://ishin95.exblog.jp/   Designer：平松創三 SOZO HIRAMATSU   Brand：ライフスタイルブランド EBI

160

BAG - nassensan TOTTE BAG 〈twist〉

Brand : nassensan　　　Designer : シミズダニヤスノブ　Yasunobu Shimizudani　　http://www.nassensan.jp, http://www.jubi-lee.com

BAG - nassensan TOTTE BAG 〈ミッドナイト〉

http://www.nassensan.jp   Designer：方波見史朗 Shiro Katabami   Brand : nassensan

BAG - nassensan TOTTE BAG

Brand : nassensan   Designer : 方波見史朗 Shiro Katabami, シミズダニヤスノブ Yasunobu Shimizudani, 吉井隆祐 Ryusuke Yoshii

Photo Credit : KYOTOTO

SOCKS - 雨足 / 足袋ソックス TABI SOCKS   http://www.kyototo.jp/, http://www.3min.jp/
Brand : 京東都 KYOTOTO   Designer : スリーミン・グラフィック・アソシエイツ 3MIN. GRAPHIC ASSOCIATES

167

http://www.kyototo.jp/, http://www.3min.jp/   **EMBROIDERED PATCH -** 和片 100 洛中洛外図　和片（わっぺん）
Designer：スリーミン・グラフィック・アソシエイツ　3MIN. GRAPHIC ASSOCIATES　　Brand：京東都　KYOTOTO

168

BROOCH - ペーパーアクセサリーズ **PAPER ACCESSORIES**
Brand : beloved design   Director : 堀口秀司 Shuji Horiguchi   http://beloved-design.com

HAND TOWEL - ジャスト ルッキング タオル **JUST LOOKING TOWEL**
Brand : DESIGN AGAINST TREND   Designer：アレックス リッチ ALEX RICH   http://www.bytrico.com/designer_label/dat.html

BABY BIB - BAB

http://www.amabro.com, http://www.amdr.jp/   Designer：村上 周 MURAKAMI AMANE   Brand：amabro

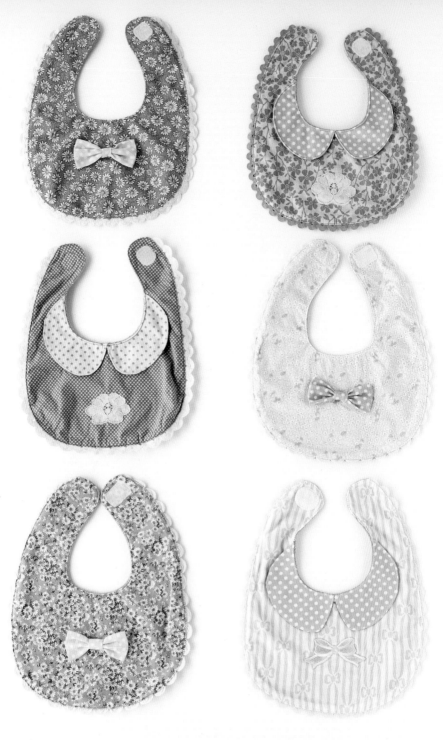

172

BABY BIB - ビブ

Brand : フェフェ fāfā   Designer : リエ, ヘレン, ミヤオカ Rie helen Miyaoka   http://www.fa-fa.co.uk, http://www.fafa-shop.com

HAIR ACCESSORY - Bow Series ヘアピン **, VERA Series** ふわふわヘアゴム **/** ふわふわピン **, Lolly Series** ヘアピン

http://www.fa-fa.co.uk, http://www.fafa-shop.com   Designer：リエ、ヘレン、ミヤオカ Rie helen Miyaoka   Brand：フェフェ fāfā

174

PHONE STRAP - ストラップ〈ウサギ, オウム, バイク, 羊, 草むらウサギ, 猫〉
Brand：アトリエ m.k.o　　Designer：鈴木美貴子 Suzuki Mikiko　　http://suzukimikiko.moo.jp/

BROOCH - ブローチ 〈カサ，白鳥，ウサギ，王冠，羊，バイオリン，シカ〉

http://suzukimikiko.moo.jp/   Designer：鈴木美貴子 Suzuki Mikiko   Brand：アトリエ m.k.o

PASS CASE, WALLET - ROUND パスケース , **ART NUME LEATHER** スリム長財布

Brand : HIRAMEKI.   Designer : takuji   http://www.e-hirameki.jp, http://sky.ap.teacup.com/takuji/

BOOK JACKET - ART NUME LEATHER ブックカバー

http://www.e-hirameki.jp, http://sky.ap.teacup.com/takuji/   Designer : takuji   Brand : HIRAMEKI.

BROOCH - 刺繍ブローチ
Brand / Designer：tamao　　http://www.tamao-world.com/

180

SKIRT - Natsuko KOZUE skirt〈波止場 , cherry〉
Designer：楜 夏子 Natsuko KOZUE   http://www17.ocn.ne.jp/˜cozupy/

182

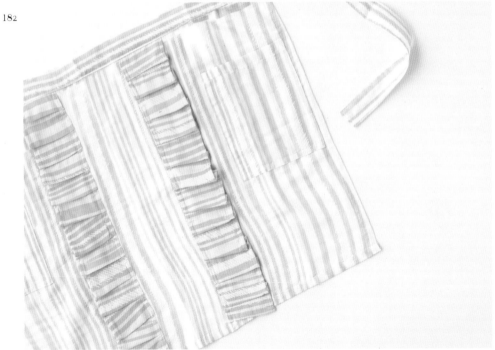

WAIST APRON - SUMAU BASE / 腰下タックエプロン
Brand : SUMAU nani IRO   Designer : SUMAU Design Team   http://www.kokka.co.jp/sumau/, http://www.itonao.com/

BAG - SUMAU KODOMO / POSTER と **BASIC POCHO** のリバーシブル手さげかばん

http://www.kokka.co.jp/sumau/, http://www.itonao.com/   Designer : SUMAU Design Team   Brand : SUMAU nani IRO

184

185

BAG - SUMAU KODOMO / ラミネートブラウンバッグ

http://www.kokka.co.jp/sumau/, http://www.itonao.com/   Designer : SUMAU Design Team   Brand : SUMAU nani IRO

186

BAG - バッグ〈フクロウと木〉
Brand : VRANA   Designer : 井上朗宏 Akihiro Inoue   http://www.vrana.jp

BAG - Recycle Market Large, Recycle Daily

http://jposh.jp, http://mmmg.net/   Designer : OH HYUN SUK   Brand : mmmg / millimeter milligram

188

SLIPPERS - CHAOS

Brand : FormlessDesign   Designer : 石橋鉄志 , 田中カォス   http://www.formlessdesign.com, http://store.novelax.jp

BAG - SEAM! ⟨Square Bag / limited color - front⟩
Brand : PANTALOON   Designer : パンタロン PANTALOON   http://www.pantaloon.org/

BAG - SEAM! ⟨Square Bag / limited color - back⟩

BAG - SEAM! ⟨Round Bag / limited color⟩

Brand : PANTALOON   Designer : パンタロン PANTALOON   http://www.pantaloon.org/

BROOCH - SEAM! 〈3dots brooch, 2sides brooch〉

http://www.pantaloon.org/   Designer : パンタロン PANTALOON   Brand : PANTALOON

BAG - Serif Tote Bag
Brand : Little Factory   Designer : Chifun Wong   http://littlefactory.com/, http://the-item.com/

CLUTCH BAG - 10th Collection 〈ravioli series - clutch bag / navy, white, black, beige〉

http://enamel.co.jp   Brand / Designer : enamel.

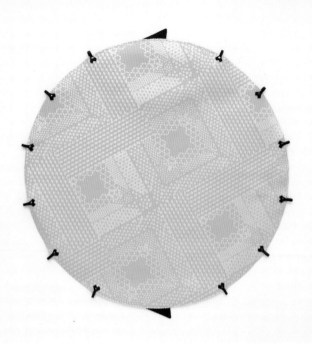

BAG - 10th Collection 〈ravioli series - bag / M beige〉
Brand / Designer : enamel.   http://enamel.co.jp

Credit

商品提供者・販売店一覧

P008-009   **Submitter : SPACE-BA store**

http://www.spacebastore.com/

Shop : LOFT (http://www.loft.co.jp/) , 東急ハンズ (http://www.tokyu-hands.co.jp/)

P010-011   **Submitter : drop around**

http://www.droparound.com/

Original Shop : drop around online store (http://www.droparound.com/)

Shop : DELFONICS (http://www.delfonics.com/) ,

恵文社一乗寺店 (http://www.keibunsha-books.com/)

P012   **Submitter : コッカ cocca**

http://www.cocca.ne.jp/

Original Shop : cocca (http://www.cocca.ne.jp/)

P013-018   **Submitter : BOX & NEEDLE**

http://boxandneedle.com

Address : 〒 158-0094 東京都世田谷区玉川 3-12-11 Tel : 03-6411-7886

Original Shop : BOX & NEEDLE 二子玉川店 (http://boxandneedle.com)

P019-021   **Submitter : yuruliku DESIGN**

Original Shop : BUNGU AND DESIGN yuruliku (http://www.yuruliku.com/b-and-d/) ,

yuruliku Online Shop (http://yuruliku.shop-pro.jp/)

P022-029   **Submitter : Number 62**

http://www.number62.jp/

Shop : CIBONE (http://cibone.com/) ,

スパイラルマーケット (http://www.spiral.co.jp/) ,

スーベニアフロムトーキョー (http://www.souvenirfromtokyo.jp/)

P030-031   **Submitter : Titto**

http://www.titto.info/

Shop：MoMA Design Store (http://www.momastore.jp/) ,

伊勢丹新宿店イセタンガール (http://www.isetan.co.jp/) ,

グリーンレーベル リラクシング 町田東急ツインズ店 (http://www.green-label-relaxing.jp/)

P032-033   **Submitter : 株式会社スペースジョイ SPACE JOY CORPORATION**

http://www.space-joy.co.jp/

Original Shop : J.[posh] 吉祥寺 (http://www.jposh.jp/)

P034-037   **Submitter : 梢 夏子 Natsuko KOZUE**

http://www17.ocn.ne.jp/~cozupy/

Shop : 恵文社一乗寺店 (http://www.keibunsha-books.com/) ,

alphabet (http://www.alphabet123.com/) ,

UGUiSU (http://uguisu.ocnk.net/)

P038-039   **Submitter : 株式会社アーテファクトリー Artefactory INC.**

http://www.artefactory.co.jp/

Original Shop : アートショップ・ピエボ (http://pievo.artgene.net)

P040-043　**Submitter：川島枝梨花　Erica kawashima**

http://tokyoparadise.jp

Shop：Ékoca（http://www.ekoca.com/），恵文社一乗寺店（http://www.keibunsha-books.com/），
COOKCOOP（http://www.cookcoop.com/），スパイラルマーケット（http://www.spiral.co.jp/），
SOMA JAPON（Tel / Fax：0287-62-5320）

P044-045　**Submitter：かみの工作所 / 福永紙工 株式会社**

http://www.kaminokousakujo.jp

Shop（PIECE OF CAKE CARD）：Minette（http://www.minette72.net/index.html）

Shop（折水引 ORIMIZUHIKI）：LIVING MOTIF（http://www.livingmotif.com），
金沢 21 世紀美術館（http://www.kanazawa21.jp/），store 1894（http://mimt.jp/index.html）

P046　**Submitter：Nendesign**

http://www.nendesign.net

Mail：info@nendesign.net

P047　**Submitter：twelvetone**

http://twelvetone.jp/

Mail：office@twelvetone.jp

Shop：shop DETAIL（http://www.detail.co.jp/）

P048　**Submitter：やまさき薫　Kaoru Yamasaki**

http://www.gruescope.com/, http://yamasakikaoru.blog113.fc2.com/

Shop：にじ画廊（http://www12.ocn.ne.jp/%7Eniji/），6 次元（http://www.6jigen.com/）

P049　**Submitter：UTRECHT**

http://www.utrecht.jp/

Original Shop：UTRECHT（http://www.utrecht.jp/）

Shop：MUJI 銀座松坂屋 MUJI BOOKS
（Address：東京都中央区銀座 6-10-1 松坂屋銀座店本館 B2F　Tel：03-5537-0757）

P050　**Submitter：かみみの**

http://www.kamimino.jp/

P051　**Submitter：トリル**

http://www5d.biglobe.ne.jp/~calico/10-trill/trill-00top.htm

Shop：月兎社 （http://www5d.biglobe.ne.jp/~calico/index.html），FALL（http://fall-gallery.com/），
ひぐらし文庫（http://higurasibooks.blog.so-net.ne.jp/），iTohen（http://www.skky.info/index.html），
Calo（http://www.calobookshop.com/），beyer（http://www.beyerbooks-pl.us/），
恵文社一乗寺店（http://www.keibunsha-books.com/），Lykkelig（http://www.lykkelig.jp/）

P052　**Submitter：yuruliku DESIGN**

Original Shop：BUNGU AND DESIGN yuruliku（http://www.yuruliku.com/b-and-d/），
yuruliku Online Shop（http://yuruliku.shop-pro.jp/）

P053　**Submitter：トリコ インターナショナル**

http://www.bytrico.com/

Original Shop：トリコ インターナショナル（http://www.bytrico.com/item/hungming/HM02.html）

P054-055 Submitter : マーブル・アンド・コー **MARBLE & Co.**
http://www.marble-and-co.com/
Shop : ブランドサイト参照（http://www.marble-and-co.com/）

P056-058 Submitter : **sallbo design**
http://www.sallbo.com/
Mail : sallbo@gmail.com
Original Shop : http://sallboshop.com/
Shop : 伊勢丹新宿店，CIBONE AOYAMA

P059-061 Submitter : 株式会社スペースジョイ **SPACE JOY CORPORATION**
http://www.space-joy.co.jp/
Original Shop : J.[posh] 自由が丘（http://www.jposh.jp/）

P064-065 Submitter : 有限会社ランドスケーププロダクツ
Original Shop : Playmountain（http://www.landscape-products.net/PM_index.html）

P066-070 Submitter : バーズワーズ **BIRDS' WORDS**
http://www.birds-words.com/
Original Shop : BIRDS' WORDS GALLERY（http://www.birds-words.com/contact/）

P071 Submitter : 株式会社 能作 **NOUSAKU CORPORATION**
http://www.nousaku.co.jp/
Original Shop : 日本橋三越内「高岡・能作」（http://www.nousaku.co.jp/）

P072-075 Submitter : **atelier de la paix**
http://homepage.mac.com/makoto46/
Shop : biotope（http://www.biotope.biz/），
黄色い鳥器店（http://www.kiiroi-tori.com/），
B・B・B POTTERS（http://www.bbbpotters.com/），
mokodi（http://www.mokodi.com/），
GARB DOMINGO（http://www.garbdomingo.com/）

P076-079 Submitter : **ON ZA LINE**
http://www.onzaline.com/

P080-081 Submitter : **Chifun Wong**
http://littlefactory.com
Original Shop : http://littlefactory.com/shop

P082-083 Submitter : **THOUSAND LEAVES**
http://www.thousandleaves.jp/
Shop : セレクトグッズショップ四月（http://shigatsu.jp）

P084-085 Submitter : 土井朋子 **Tomoko Doi**
http://www.doitomo.com/
Shop : バーデンバーデン（http://www.badenbaden.jp/）

P086   **Submitter：キコ / 株式会社ネロリ　QUICO / NEROLI Co.,Ltd.**
http://www.quico.jp/
Original Shop：QUICO (http://www.quico.jp/)

P087   **Submitter：歩陶房　po-to-bo**
http://po-to-bo.com
Original Shop : po-to-bo (http://po-to-bo.com)

P088-089   **Submitter：楽土　Raku-do**
http://raku-do.net/
Mail : info@raku-do.net
Shop : neutron ニュートロン (http://www.neutron-kyoto.com/) ,
All About スタイルストア (http://stylestore.allabout.co.jp/) ,
森陶器館 (http://www.moritoukikan.jp/)

P090-092   **Submitter : cocoo natural home decor**
http://cocoo.jp
Mail : info@cocoo.jp

P093-095   **Submitter：かみみの**
http://www.kamimino.jp/

P096-097   **Submitter：ジジ　gg**
http://shop.lucky-clover.jp/
Shop：ジジ　gg (http://shop.lucky-clover.jp/)

P098-099   **Submitter：株式会社 キハラ　KIHARA INC.**
http://www.e-kihara.co.jp/

P100-101   **Submitter : Tas-ka**
http://www.tas-ka.nl/, http://www.collectedbytas-ka.com/
Shop : DESPERADO (http://desperadoweb.net/)

P102   **Submitter : Nendesign**
http://www.nendesign.net
Mail : info@nendesign.net

P103   **Submitter：株式会社マック　MAQ inc.**
http://www.maq.co.jp/
Tel : 03-5411-2646
Shop : ブランドサイト参照 (http://www.gba-project.com/)

P104-105   **Submitter：トリコ インターナショナル**
http://www.bytrico.com/
Original Shop：トリコ インターナショナル (http://www.bytrico.com/item/donnawilson/DW58.html,
http://www.bytrico.com/item/donnawilson/DW74.html,
http://www.bytrico.com/item/donnawilson/DW50.html)

P106-107 Submitter：コッカ cocca
http://www.cocca.ne.jp/
Original Shop：cocca（http://www.cocca.ne.jp/）

P108 Submitter：the.
http://www.thinkofthe.com
Original Shop：http://www.thinkofthe.com
Shop：http://www.arktrading.jp/

P109 Submitter：twelvetone
http://twelvetone.jp/
Mail：office@twelvetone.jp
Shop：shop DETAIL（http://www.detail.co.jp/）

P110 Submitter：かみみの
http://www.kamimino.jp/

P111 Submitter：かみの工作所 / 福永紙工 株式会社
http://www.kaminokousakujo.jp
Shop：LIVING MOTIF（http://www.livingmotif.com），
CLASKA Gallery & Shop "DO" 渋谷店（http://www.claska.com），
森アーツセンターミュージアムショップ（http://www.macmuseumshop.com）

P112-113 Submitter：株式会社オプスデザイン
Mail：contact@opus-design.jp
Shop：prideli graphic lab（http://www.prideli.net/）

P114-115 Submitter：有限会社アートニクス creative works ARTNIKS
http://www.artniks.jp/
Shop：キャトル・セゾン 全店（http://www.quatresaisons.co.jp/），
イノブン 天満橋店（http://www.inobun.co.jp/），KuLaSu season なんばパークス店（http://kulasu.jp/）

P116-117 Submitter：株式会社 ディアール DR.co.,ltd.
http://soapylove.dr-jp.com/
Original Shop：オフィシャルサイト（http://soapylove.dr-jp.com/）
Shop：CIBONE 自由が丘店（http://cibone.com/），
miomio コレド日本橋店（http://www.miomio-web.com/shoplist/），KITSON（http://shopkitson.jp/information.html）

P118-122 Submitter：amabro / 村上美術株式会社 MURAKAMI BIJYUTSU Co.Ltd.
Original Shop：amabro online store（http://www.amabro.com）

P123 Submitter：collex
http://www.collex.jp/
Original Shop：collex LIVING, collex ONLINE SHOP（http://shop.collex.jp/?mode=grp&gid=76297）

P124-128 Submitter：コッカ cocca
http://www.cocca.ne.jp/
Original Shop：cocca（http://www.cocca.ne.jp/）

P129   **Submitter：福井優子**

http://progressivecandle.blog21.fc2.com/

Shop：札幌スタイルショップ（http://www.city.sapporo.jp/keizai/sapporo-style/ss-shop.html），

山卜 小笠原商店 〜新千歳空港 国際線内（ブログアドレス：http://ameblo.jp/yamato-ogasawara/），

ConceptBlue コンセプトブルー（http://www.conceptblue.jp/）

P130-133   **Submitter：ライフスタイルブランド EBI**

http://ebidesign.jp/

Shop：Aquvii（http://www.aquvii.com），Coquette（http://www.coquette.jp/index.html），

poooL（http://www.poool.jp）

p134-139   **Submitter：点と線模様製作所 ten to sen**

http://www.tentosen.info

Shop：東急ハンズ名古屋（http://nagoya.tokyu-hands.co.jp/），木木（http://kigi.cloud-bldg.jp/），

手紙舎（http://www.tegamisha.com/）

P142-143   **Submitter：HIPOTA**

http://www8.plala.or.jp/hipotastitch/

Shop：バーデンバーデン（http://www.badenbaden.jp/）

P144-145   **Submitter：ai ／布川愛子**

http://www.nice-nice-nice.com

Mail：info@nice-nice-nice.com

Shop：shop Rallye（http://www.rallye-kanazawa.com/shop/home.html），ハイジ（http://heidi-home.com），

gallo the living（http://www.gallotheliving.jp），EIN SHOP（http://www.einshop.jp）

P146-149   **Submitter：giraffe**

www.giraffe-tie.com

Address：東京都渋谷区猿楽町29-9 ヒルサイドテラス D-5　Tel：03-5941-5675

Original Shop：giraffe（http://giraffe-tie.com/）

Shop：PASS THE BATON MARUNOUCHI,

PASS THE BATON OMOTESANDO（http://www.pass-the-baton.com）

P150-151   **Submitter：コッカ cocca**

http://www.cocca.ne.jp/

Original Shop：cocca（http://www.cocca.ne.jp/）

P152-153   **Submitter：petitricot**

http://www5f.biglobe.ne.jp/~p-tricot/

Shop：セレクトショップ 京（http://www.selectshopkyo.com/）

P154-155   **Submitter：キコ ／ 株式会社ネロリ QUICO / NEROLI Co.,Ltd.**

http://www.quico.jp/

Original Shop：QUICO（http://www.quico.jp/）

P156-157   **Submitter：collex**

http://www.collex.jp/

Original Shop：collex LIVING, collex ONLINE SHOP（http://shop.collex.jp/?mode=grp&gid=76297）

P158   Submitter : 歩陶房　po-to-bo

http://po-to-bo.com
Original Shop : po-to-bo (http://po-to-bo.com)

P159   Submitter : ライフスタイルブランド **EBI**

http://ebidesign.jp/
Shop : Aquvii (http://www.aquvii.com) ,
Coquette (http://www.coquette.jp/index.html) ,
poooL (http://www.poool.jp)

P160-161   Submitter : **inoui**

http://inoui-world.com
Shop : ASSEMBLAGE (http://www1k.mesh.ne.jp/assemblage/) ,
poooL (http://www.poool.jp) ,
雑貨店おやつ (http://www.o-ya-tsu.com)

P162-165   Submitter : **nassensan**

http://www.nassensan.jp
Shop : DESPERADO (http://desperadoweb.net) ,
オオロラ舎 (http://www.aurora-sha.com)

P166-167   Submitter : 株式会社ドゥオモ　**DUOMO Co.,Ltd.**

Shop : スーベニアフロムトーキョー (http://www.souvenirfromtokyo.jp/) ,
Tokyo's Tokyo (http://www.tokyo-airport-bldg.co.jp/shops_and_restaurants/store/299/) ,
京都デザインハウス (http://www.kyoto-dh.com/)

P168-169   Submitter : デ・アンド・コー　**de + Co**

http://beloved-design.com
Shop : ブランドサイト参照

P170   Submitter : トリコ インターナショナル

http://www.bytrico.com/
Original Shop : トリコ インターナショナル (http://www.bytrico.com/item/dat/DAT41.html)

P171   Submitter : amabro / 村上美術株式会社　**MURAKAMI BIJYUTSU Co.Ltd.**

Original Shop : amabro online store (http://www.amabro.com)

P172-173   Submitter : 株式会社テル・ア・テール　**Tell a Tale**

Original Shop : fafa オンラインショップ (http://www.fafa-shop.com), fafa 福岡 PARCO

P174-175   Submitter : アトリエ **m.k.o**

http://suzukimikiko.moo.jp/
Mail : minazuki30@yahoo.co.jp

P176-177   Submitter : **HIRAMEKI.**

http://www.e-hirameki.jp

P178-179   **Submitter : tamao**

http://www.tamao-world.com/

Shop：スーベニアフロムトーキョー（http://www.souvenirfromtokyo.jp），

marble-sud 恵比寿本店（http://www.marble-sud.com/），

カオリノモリ ラフォーレ原宿店（http://www.kaorinomori.jp）

P180-181   **Submitter : 梢 夏子 Natsuko KOZUE**

http://www17.ocn.ne.jp/~cozupy/

Shop：恵文社一乗寺店（http://www.keibunsha-books.com/），

alphabet（http://www.alphabet123.com/），

UGUiSU（http://uguisu.ocnk.net/）

P182-185   **Submitter : 有限会社アートニクス creative works ARTNIKS**

http://www.artniks.jp/

Shop：キャトル・セゾン 全店（http://www.quatresaisons.co.jp/），

イノブン 天満橋店（http://www.inobun.co.jp/），

KuLaSu season なんばパークス店（http://kulasu.jp/）

P186   **Submitter : VRANA**

http://www.vrana.jp

P187   **Submitter : 株式会社スペースジョイ SPACE JOY CORPORATION**

http://www.space-joy.co.jp/

Original Shop：J.[posh] 吉祥寺（http://www.jposh.jp/）

P188-189   **Submitter : FormlessDesign**

http://www.formlessdesign.com

Original Shop：novelax store online（http://store.novelax.jp）

Shop：密売東京（http://www.mitsubai.com）

P190-193   **Submitter : PANTALOON**

http://www.pantaloon.org/

Shop：OUTBOUND（http://outbound.to/），

graf（http://www.graf-d3.com/），

Töölö（http://www.def-company.co.jp/toolo/index.html）

P194   **Submitter : Chifun Wong**

http://littlefactory.com

Original Shop：http://littlefactory.com/shop/

P195-197   **Submitter : enamel.**

http://enamel.co.jp

Original Shop：only tuesdays（http://enamel.co.jp）

夢みるデザインプロダクト

2010 年 9 月 23 日　初版第一刷発行

アートディレクション・デザイン：石田崇仁（NAIJEL GRAPH）
撮影：水野聖二
クッキーデザイン［カバー、章扉］：cookieboy
翻訳［序文］：アールアイシー出版
企画・編集：石井早耶香

発行人：籔内康一
発行所：株式会社ビー・エヌ・エヌ新社
　　　　〒 150-0022
　　　　東京都渋谷区恵比寿南一丁目 20 番 6 号
　　　　fax：03-5725-1511
　　　　e-mail：info@bnn.co.jp

印刷・製本：株式会社廣済堂